# DINOSAURS

First published in Canada by Whitecap Books
351 Lynn Avenue, North Vancouver, British Columbia, V7J 2C4

Text and illustration copyright © Random House Australia Pty
Ltd, 2000

ISBN 1-55285-065-X

Children's Publisher: Linsay Knight
Series Editor: Marie-Louise Taylor
Managing Editor: Derek Barton
Art Directors: Carolyn Hewitson and Vicky Short
Design concept: Stan Lamond
Production Manager: Linda Watchorn

Illustrators: Kevin Stead, pages 6–7, 10–19, 22–31, 34–43, 48–51;
Jenny Black, pages 8–9, 20–21, 32–33, 44–47, 56–57;
Spike Wademan, pages 52–55
Consultant: Robert Jones
Writer: Judith Simpson
Educational Consultant: Pamela Hook

Film separation by Pica Colour Separation Overseas Pte Ltd,
Singapore
Printed in Hong Kong by Sing Cheong Printing Co. Ltd.

When you see a word in **bold** type, you'll find its
meaning in the Glossary at the back of the book.

# DINOSAURS

Consultant **Robert Jones**
Illustrators **Kevin Stead,**
**Jenny Black & Spike Wademan**

WHITECAP
B O O K S

# CONTENTS

# CONTENTS

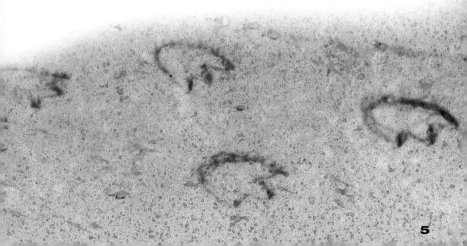

# Hunter and hunted

*More than 70 million years ago, two huge and heavy dinosaurs fought fiercely. The hunter (left) was* Tyrannosaurus rex. *The hunted (right) was* Triceratops.

## DIVERSE DINOSAURS

Dinosaurs were a large and diverse group of **reptiles**. Scientists have put together the story of how they lived from many bits of **fossil** evidence. These include fossilised bones, eggs, dung and footprints; and imprints of skin, leaves and feathers. We know a lot about *Tyrannosaurus rex* and *Triceratops* but no single complete **skeleton** of either has yet been found.

cycads

## Tyrannosaurus rex

**Name:** Tyrannosaurus rex (tie-RAN-oh-SORE-us)

**Family:** Tyrannosaurids

**Lived when:** Late Cretaceous period

**Lived where:** North America, Asia

**Length:** 12 metres (40 feet)

**Favourite food:** Meat freshly killed or scavenged from dead bodies

## LOOK
### AGAIN!

*Triceratops'* neck **frill** was edged with bony studs to help protect the animal.

conifers

horsetails

ferns

# Back to the Triassic

*Dinosaurs first appeared on Earth more than 225 million years ago and were around for about 160 million years. The Mesozoic era, in which they lived, was divided into three periods—Triassic, Jurassic and Cretaceous.*

## TRIASSIC LANDSCAPE

Not all types of dinosaurs lived at the same time. As one **species** was dying out, it made room for another to **evolve**. The climate in the Triassic period (251 to 205 million years ago) was mild and there was plenty of vegetation to feed plant-eaters such as *Plateosaurus* (far back). There were **ginkgos** and tree-fern forests, **conifers** and **cycads**, **horsetails** and medium-sized ferns. *Herrerasaurus* (left) was a meat-eater. It shared the creatures that could be hunted as prey with *Coelophysis* (middle) and other meat-eating dinosaurs. The three animals near the water were not dinosaurs. Triassic turtles and crocodiles looked rather like the turtles and crocodiles that are still around today. The **dicynodont**, which was a medium-sized mammal-like creature, became **extinct**.

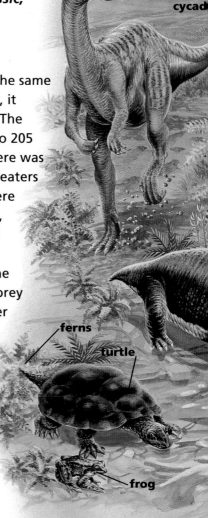

conifers

cycad

ferns

turtle

frog

**LOOK AGAIN!**

Which animals in this picture are not dinosaurs? Some are still around today.

tree-ferns

horsetails

dicynodont

crocodile

furry mammals

9

# Meet the meat-eaters

*Dinosaurs evolved from a group of reptiles called **thecodonts**. All the very first dinosaurs were **carnivores**. This meant that they ate meat and hunted other animals in order to survive.*

## HUNTERS ON THE RUN

*Coelophysis* is one of the oldest dinosaurs in the world known from whole skeletons. Scientists have found the fossilised bones of many bodies. These small dinosaurs ran swiftly on strong hind legs. *Herrerasaurus* (back) was probably too big for *Coelophysis* to attack. *Coelophysis* used its sharp teeth to tear the skin of its **prey**. It was particularly good at dodging scratches, bites and kicks from its victims. Sometimes dinosaurs left footprints in damp sand or soft mud. From these **trackways** scientists can work out how many animals were running and how fast they were going.

## LOOK AGAIN!

How many species of dinosaur have left their footprints in the sand?

# Coelophysis

**Name:** *Coelophysis*
(SEE-loh-FIE-sis)

**Family:** Coelurosaurs

**Lived when:** Late
Triassic period

**Lived where:** North
America (United States)

**Length:** 3 metres (10 feet)

**Favourite food:** Insects,
lizard-like reptiles,
other small dinosaurs
and possibly fish

*Herrerasaurus* was
also a meat-eater.

flexible neck

narrow jaw

Some meat-
eating dinosaurs
hunted in packs,
running their
victims down.

# Born to run!

*All dinosaurs moved with their legs tucked underneath their bodies. The shape of the hipbone divided them into two groups.* Saurischia *were lizard-hipped;* Ornithischia *were bird-hipped (see pages 52–55).*

## TOP RUNNERS

The shape, size and position of dinosaurs' hipbones supported the weight of their bodies. They were able to move more quickly and easily than other creatures on the Earth at the same time. Dinosaurs' lungs and breathing worked just like crocodiles' lungs and breathing today. This meant that they could be active for longer periods of time. *Saurischia* are subdivided into two more groups—**sauropods** and **theropods**. Sauropods were **quadrupedal**, which means they moved on four legs. Theropods, such as *Coelophysis*, were **bipedal** and ran on two long back legs. Their short front legs were free to grasp prey. Their fingers ended in large, sharp claws.

tail

**The muscles of a dinosaur worked like the muscles of other animals with backbones.**

ankle joint

# MODELLING MUSCLES

After a dinosaur died, the soft parts of its body rotted away. The hard parts—bones, teeth and claws—were sometimes fossilised. Impressions of skin and footprints have also been found. Scientists study the bones and work out how the joints fitted together. They also compare living animals with dinosaurs to see where muscles were attached and how they moved.

**Many small bones called vertebrae fitted together to form the neck, backbone and tail.**

**A flexible neck supported a small head.**

**neck**

**backbone**

**hip bone**

**muscle of upper forelimb**

**Ribs formed a cage to protect the heart and lungs.**

**strong claw**

**elbow joint**

**Dinosaur skin was scaly like the skin of a reptile.**

# Dino guts!

*All animals must be able to digest food to take the goodness from it. The way in which carnivores (meat-eaters) digest their food is different from the way in which **herbivores** (plant-eaters) do.*

## WARM BLOOD OR COLD?

Dinosaur experts argue about whether dinosaurs were warm-blooded like birds and mammals or cold-blooded like reptiles and amphibians. Supporters of the warm-blooded theory say that dinosaurs were much too active to have cold blood. They also say that the fine structure of dinosaurs' bones is like the bones of warm-blooded creatures alive today. The food an animal eats controls its level of energy. Supporters of the cold-blooded theory say that a large dinosaur could not have eaten enough in a day to live the life of a warm-blooded creature. Some think it possible that the huge plant-eaters were cold-blooded while the smaller meat-eaters had warm blood.

cloaca

# DIGESTING MEAT

Scientists can tell what a dinosaur has been eating from remains found in the stomach of fossilised animals and dung. Sometimes skeletons of **predators** are found with their prey still in their clutches. Carnivorous dinosaurs ate anything they could catch and some also fed on dead and rotting flesh. Meat is easier to digest than plants and the dinosaurs that lived on it had simpler digestive systems than the plant-eaters. Meat-eaters did not need **bacteria** (tiny organisms) in their stomachs to break down their food.

**sharp teeth to cut up meat**

**trachea**

**oesophagus**

**lungs**

**heart**

**kidney**

**stomach**

**intestines**

## LOOK AGAIN!

Compare the length of the intestines with those of a plant-eater on pages 24–25.

15

# Like us— bipedal

*One species of the earliest dinosaurs was something of a misfit. Its hipbone looked much the same as the later bird-hipped dinosaurs. But all bird-hipped dinosaurs ate plants and this animal was a meat-eater.*

## EAT AND BE EATEN

The unusual theropod that was neither bird-hipped nor lizard-hipped was called *Herrerasaurus*. It hunted **rhynchosaurs**, thecodont reptiles and other dinosaurs, sneaking up on them in the moist Triassic forests. But predators could also become prey. Sometimes crocodile-like reptiles pounced on *Herrerasaurus* as it paused at the water's edge to drink.

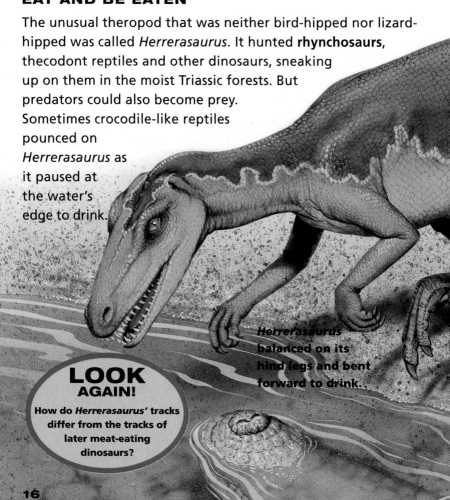

*Herrerasaurus balanced on its hind legs and bent forward to drink.*

## LOOK AGAIN!

How do *Herrerasaurus'* tracks differ from the tracks of later meat-eating dinosaurs?

# Huge herbivores

*Herbivores began to emerge during the Triassic period. These large animals lived in herds. They ate only plants and competed with one another for the available greenery.*

## WALKING FOR WEIGHT

*Plateosaurus* was a lizard-hipped dinosaur. It had a long neck and a small head for the size of its heavy body. Its front legs were shorter than its thick back legs but it usually walked on all fours to support its great weight. *Plateosaurus* could also walk on two legs, a useful way to reach up for food. Its teeth were specially shaped for shredding tough plants.

**The tail was used for balance.**

## Plateosaurus

**Name:** *Plateosaurus*
(PLAT-ee-oh-SORE-us)

**Family:** Plateosaurids (a **prosauropod,** a forerunner of the sauropods)

**Lived when:** Late Triassic period

**Lived where:** Europe (Germany, France, Switzerland, England)

**Length:** 7 metres (23 feet)

**Favourite food:** Soft plants

# Back to the Jurassic

*In the Jurassic period (205 to 141 million years ago) more rain fell and dense forests grew. They fed gigantic, plant-eating dinosaurs. Also many species of meat-eating dinosaurs evolved.*

## JURASSIC LANDSCAPE

Now forests of cycads, normal-sized conifers and very tall conifers increased in area. *Stegosaurus* (front), the plated dinosaur with the spiky tail, was a most unusual dinosaur. *Allosaurus* (middle), the terrifying theropod, killed other dinosaurs larger than itself. *Apatosaurus* (far back), a sauropod, ate vast quantities of vegetation. The cooler climate and plentiful food allowed many other creatures to thrive as well as dinosaurs. They included flying **pterosaurs**, small furry rat-like mammals and new insects. *Archaeopteryx* (AR-kee-OP-ter-iks) appeared, the forerunner of the birds.

## LOOK AGAIN!

How does this vary from the Triassic scene on pages 8–9? What new creatures are there?

pterosaurs

*Archaeopteryx*

# Eat to live or live to eat?

*When herds of Jurassic giants moved, the earth shook. A full-grown* Apatosaurus *weighed up to 30 tonnes—the weight of about five adult elephants.* Apatosaurus *ate constantly to feed its great bulk.*

## BUILT FOR BULK

*Apatosaurus* was similar in shape to *Brachiosaurus* and other sauropods. Its tiny head, set on the end of a long, slender neck, was very small in comparison with the size of the rest of its body. Its thick legs, like the pillars of a building, supported its heavy midsection. The long tail tapered to a thin whiplash, which could be flicked at attackers. *Apatosaurus* was once known as *Brontosaurus*, which means 'thunder lizard'. *Apatosaurus* means 'deceptive reptile', but it is unlikely that this huge herbivore could ever have hidden anywhere.

**huge hipbones to carry enormous weight**

**Tail vertebrae taper and turn the long, thin, flexible end into a defensive weapon.**

# Apatosaurus

**Name:** *Apatosaurus*
(uh-PAT-oh-SORE-us)

**Family:** Diplodocids

**Lived when:** Late Jurassic period

**Lived where:** North America

**Length:** 21 metres (70 feet)

**Favourite food:** Plants

Small teeth are designed to rake in plant matter.

Vertebrae were huge and hollow, making them light and strong.

long neck for raising the head high into the treetops

large shoulder bone to support thick foreleg

neck thickens at base

## LOOK AGAIN!

*Apatosaurus* had short fat toes that looked rather like the toes of elephants.

# Plant-eating giants

*The teeth of herbivorous sauropod dinosaurs were not designed for chewing. The creatures ripped vast quantities of leaves and twigs off trees and bushes and swallowed the roughly torn-off pieces.*

## FOOD PROCESSING

Plant-eaters needed a strong digestive system to process their food and slowly release its goodness. As well as **gastroliths** (stones) in their stomachs, dinosaurs must have had tiny organisms in their intestines to break down the **cellulose** (plant fibres) just as herbivorous animals such as rhinoceroses do today. The digestive system of herbivorous dinosaurs made sure that every bit of the goodness in the food was used. It needed to be to keep these enormous animals going.

Sauropods swallowed small stones to help them digest food. The constant movement in their gut of these smooth pebbles, called gastroliths, crushed food into an easily digested paste.

**ACTUAL SIZE GASTROLITH**

# INTESTINES INSIDE

These big animals were too heavy to walk on their hind legs only and it is unlikely that dinosaurs of this size ever moved very quickly. By the end of the Jurassic period, these browsing giants had had a major impact on the Earth's vegetation. Remember that plant-eaters need a much larger and longer intestine to digest their food than meat-eaters do. The shape of the hipbone in the large sauropods meant that this great length of intestine was carried well forward in the body.

Microbes help to digest food.

narrow intestines

trachea

Strong stomach wall muscles squeeze food.

Muscles help to push food down to the stomach.

lungs

heart

Food travels down the oesophagus.

Plant food is reduced to a thick paste.

gastroliths

## LOOK AGAIN!

What can you see in this dinosaur's stomach that tells you it is a plant-eater?

# Deadly predator

*Allosaurus was the most successful killer on Earth during the Jurassic period. It hunted animals much larger and heavier than itself. It may also have eaten the carcasses of creatures already dead.*

## KILLING MACHINE

*Allosaurus* probably stalked its prey like a lion and then pounced with deadly speed. It could bring down giant sauropods, especially if they were young or weak. The skull of *Allosaurus* was the perfect meat-eating machine. Its jaws were large and could open very wide. Its teeth were serrated, notched along the edges like steak knives.

strong tail held off the ground for balance

large powerful back legs

## Allosaurus

**Name:** *Allosaurus* (AL-oh-SORE-us)

**Family:** Allosaurids

**Lived when:** Late Jurassic period

**Lived where:** North America

**Length:** 11–12 metres (35–40 feet)

**Favourite food:** Any animal it could kill

### LOOK AGAIN!

The angle of the teeth in the jaw show that this animal was a meat-eater.

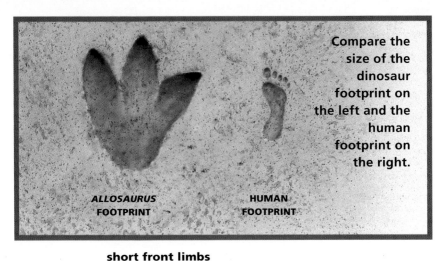

Compare the size of the dinosaur footprint on the left and the human footprint on the right.

**ALLOSAURUS FOOTPRINT**

**HUMAN FOOTPRINT**

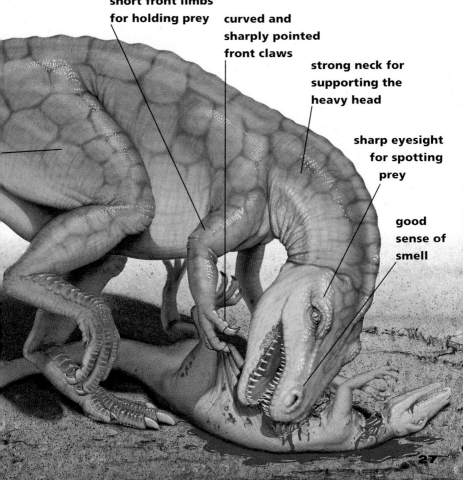

short front limbs for holding prey

curved and sharply pointed front claws

strong neck for supporting the heavy head

sharp eyesight for spotting prey

good sense of smell

# The 'plated' reptile

*Stegosaurus, the reptile with bony plates along its back, lived in the Jurassic period. It was a bird-hipped dinosaur that walked on all fours and ate only plants.*

## SHOWING BACKBONE

No bony plates have ever been found attached to a *Stegosaurus'* skeleton, so no-one is quite sure how they were arranged. It had a small head and a tiny brain. For a while, some wrongly believed that there was a second brain in the animal's hip. *Stegosaurus* ate plants that grew near the ground and did not compete much with other dinosaurs for food. Instead of teeth at the front of its jaw, it had a beak that chopped vegetation.

*Stegosaurus* **was not an agile animal and moved quite slowly.**

The spikes on *Stegosaurus'* tail could inflict horrible injuries on its predators.

The plates were filled with blood vessels that ran underneath the skin.

Scientists are still arguing about why *Stegosaurus* had bony plates along its back. Were they to help it defend itself? Or did they help to keep the animal warm or cool?

From side on, *Stegosaurus* sloped steeply front and back.

The tail ended in two pairs of long spikes.

# Stegosaurus

**Name:** *Stegosaurus* (STEG-oh-SORE-us)

**Family:** Stegosaurids

**Lived when:** Late Jurassic period

**Lived where:** North America

**Length:** 6–7 metres (20–24 feet)

**Favourite food:** Plants near the ground

a very small brain set
in a small head

The heart pumped
blood to the brain,
which was 7.5 metres
(25 feet) above it.

neck

Treetop leaves and
twigs had to travel a
long way from the
dinosaur's mouth to
its stomach.

thicker neck
at base

## JURASSIC GIANT

*Brachiosaurus* was 16 metres (52 feet) high and
weighed up to 77 tonnes. At first scientists thought
that this immense sauropod spent most of its time in
water. They believed that the water would support its
huge body and take the strain off its legs. They also
believed that because *Brachiosaurus'* nostrils were on top of
its head, they might have acted like a snorkel. A human being
can only snorkel to a depth of about 2 metres (7 feet). So the
experts soon realised that the water pressure would have
made it impossible for *Brachiosaurus* to breathe air through
its nostrils while underwater because of the distance
between its nose and its lungs—about 7 metres
(23 feet). We now know that *Brachiosaurus* walked on
land on four sturdy legs. Its front legs were much longer
than its back legs and its long neck and sloping back
made it look very much like a giraffe. In recent years,
bones have been discovered of dinosaurs that were
even bigger than *Brachiosaurus*.

# Long neck!

*The giant lizard-hipped, plant-eating sauropods of the Jurassic period were the largest animals that ever lived. Among them was Brachiosaurus, as tall as a four-storey building and weighing more than ten adult elephants.*

## Brachiosaurus

**Brachiosaurus is named because of its long front legs. The name means 'arm reptile'.**

**Name:** *Brachiosaurus* (BRAK-ee-oh-SORE-us)

**Family:** Brachiosaurids

**Lived when:** Late Jurassic period

**Lived where:** North America, Africa (Tanzania)

**Length:** 23 metres (75 feet)

**Favourite food:** Fresh shoots from the treetops

lungs

intestine

**The larger the animal, the more likely it was to have dull-coloured skin.**

heart

stomach

# ack to th
# Cretaceous

*During the Cretaceous period (141 to 65 million years ago), it became warmer. There were wet and dry seasons instead of summer and winter. New dinosaurs appeared to replace species that now died out.*

## CRETACEOUS LANDSCAPE

No grasses grew on the Earth throughout the whole of the Mesozoic era. But by the Cretaceous period, the huge herbivores had devoured large areas of forest and ferns. The first flowering plants, which grew and reproduced quickly, took over the cleared spaces. There were fewer horsetails, conifers and cycads. This was the age of *Tyrannosaurus rex,* but there were other large dinosaurs such as the hadrosaurs like *Anatosaurus* (back). *Ankylosaurus* (drinking) was protected by bony bumps and spikes on its body and a double-headed bony club on its tail. *Parasaurolophus* (right) had a hollow crest on its head. *Archaeopteryx* was extinct by now, but many more birds had developed. Small furry mammals increased in number.

## LOOK AGAIN!

How does this vary from the Triassic scene on pages 8–9 and the Jurassic scene on pages 20–21?

mixed conifer
forest

flowering
plants

flowering
plants

# Thumbs up!

*In the early 1800s Mary Ann Mantell found some huge fossilised teeth in Sussex, England. Her husband, Dr Gideon Mantell, thought these belonged to a giant extinct relative of South American **iguanas**.*

**The design of *Iguanodon*'s hipbone shows that it belonged to the Ornithischia group of dinosaurs.**

**LOOK AGAIN!**

What unusual front limb feature distinguished *Iguanodon* from other dinosaurs?

## FIGHTING THUMBS

Later, many nearly complete 'iguana tooth' skeletons from the early Cretaceous period were found in Europe. They showed a bird-hipped animal, which walked on its sturdy, three-toed back legs using its long tail for balance. The front legs were strong, too, but were shorter than the back ones. Larger *Iguanodons* might walk on all fours. This dinosaur had one distinctly unusual feature on its hands—a bony spike-shaped thumb. It could use this as a slashing weapon in a fight. The broad teeth that Mrs Mantell found came from the back of the jaw. They were used to chop up plants after *Iguanodon* had nipped them off with its toothless beak. Muscular cheeks stopped food falling from the sides of the mouth.

## Iguanodon

**Name:** *Iguanodon*
   (ih-GWAN-oh-DON)

**Family:** Iguanodontids

**Lived when:** Early
   Cretaceous period

**Lived where:** Europe
   (England, France,
   West Germany, Belgium,
   Spain); North America
   (United States)

**Length:** 10 metres (33 feet)

**Favourite food:** Plants

# Babysitting!

*Scientists know more about* Maiasaura *than any other dinosaur. These animals lived in very large groups, up to 10,000 animals in a herd.*

## IN THE NEST

Like all reptiles, young dinosaurs hatched from eggs. Dinosaurs' eggs were very small when compared with the size of the parents. They could not be larger because eggshells have to be thin enough for air to pass through for the developing **embryo** inside to breathe. Eggshells also have to be thin enough for the **hatchlings** to break open. *Maiasaura*'s nest sites tell us much about how hadrosaurs cared for their eggs and young. They laid their eggs in a mound of dirt and covered them with plant matter, much like crocodiles do today. The warmth of the rotting vegetation kept the eggs at the right temperature until they hatched. Parents probably stood guard over their nests to discourage egg thieves and stop other *Maiasauras* from trampling them. The hatchlings grew rapidly from about 40.5 centimetres (16 inches) to 147 centimetres (58 inches) in the first year.

## LOOK AGAIN!

*Maiasaura* laid eggs in a regular spiral pattern with a space between each egg.

Newly hatched dinosaurs were much smaller than their parents.

Parents brought food to their young.

When they were big enough, the young left the nest.

Up to twenty-five eggs were laid at a time.

A dirt mound raised the eggs above the ground.

## Maiasaura

**Name:** *Maiasaura* (MY-ah-SORE-ah)

**Family:** Hadrosaurids

**Lived when:** Late Cretaceous period

**Lived where:** North America (United States)

**Length:** 9 metres (30 feet)

**Favourite food:** Plants

# Bony armour

*Saltasaurus was one of the most successful of all the sauropods that lived in the Cretaceous period. It was protected against predators by its coating of armour.*

### STUDDED SKIN

The best defence that the Jurassic giants such as *Apatosaurus* and *Brachiosaurus* had against the meat-eaters was their size. Fully grown, they were too large for a theropod to tackle. By Cretaceous times, however, theropods had grown bigger. So what was special about *Saltasaurus,* medium-sized as dinosaurs go? From fossil remains, scientists know that *Saltasaurus* had hundreds of pea-sized bones and larger bony plates, the size of human hands, embedded in its skin. This meant that a hunting dinosaur could not get a grip when it pounced.

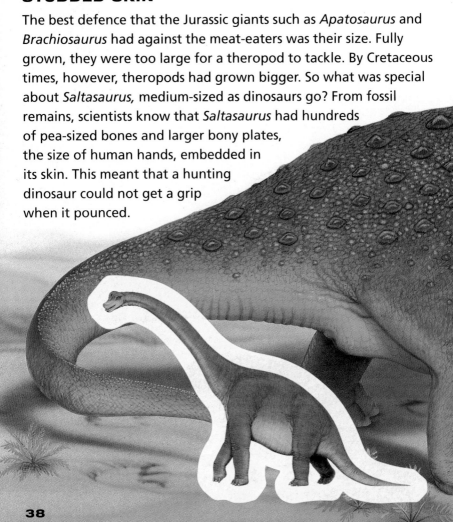

# Saltasaurus

**Name:** *Saltasaurus*
(SALT-ah-SORE-us)

**Family:** Titanosaurids

**Lived when:** Late
Cretaceous period

**Lived where:** South America
(Argentina)

**Length:** 12 metres (40 feet)

**Favourite food:** Plants

*Saltasaurus*
**was a peaceful
plant-eater.**

**The neck was
not armoured.**

*Saltasaurus*
**walked on four
sturdy legs.**

# LOOK
## AGAIN!

**Dinosaurs had eyelids like lizards, crocodiles, alligators and other present-day reptiles.**

# Dino eyes

*Eyes are soft tissue and do not survive as fossils. Scientists have no dinosaur eyes so they must study the eyes of living animals.*

## EYE OPENER

Scientists judge eye size from the size of the eye socket. In carnivorous dinosaurs these were very big. These creatures needed sharp eyesight and an acute sense of smell to track down prey. Herbivores had slightly smaller eyes. Many living reptiles do not see colours. However, birds need colour vision to recognise their species and they communicate with visual signals such as raising tails and crests. As dinosaurs were closely related to birds, it is possible that they could also see colours.

Compare the actual size human eye and the eye of a large dinosaur depicted here. Dinosaurs had no eyelashes, eyebrows or hair of any kind.

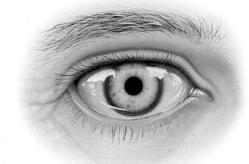

# Duckbills

*Dinosaurs' heads were all sorts of shapes and sizes. Some had bony plates for protection in head-butting contests or horns with which to ram an enemy. Others had bony bumps or crests.*

## CRESTED CREATURES

Hadrosaurs or duckbills were so called because of their broad, duck-like, toothless beak. Behind this, they had up to 300 teeth in each jaw for grinding up the plants they fed on. This group of dinosaurs had the oddest shaped heads. The reasons for such different decorations have been much discussed. Hadrosaurs' headgear probably helped them to recognise their own species when two or more lived in the same place. So males would know females of their own kind. *Parasaurolophus* males had a hollow bony crest about 1 metre (3 feet) long. Scientists think that this made their calls louder to reach distant members of the herd.

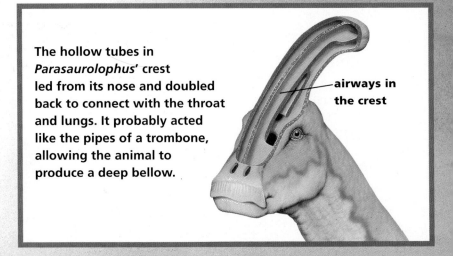

The hollow tubes in *Parasaurolophus'* crest led from its nose and doubled back to connect with the throat and lungs. It probably acted like the pipes of a trombone, allowing the animal to produce a deep bellow.

airways in the crest

Like most other land animals, dinosaurs could swim when they were forced to cross water.

## Parasaurolophus

**Name:** *Parasaurolophus* (PAIR-uh-SORE-o-LOF-us)

**Family:** Hadrosaurids

**Lived when:** Late Cretaceous period

**Lived where:** North America

**Length:** 10 metres (33 feet)

**Favourite food:** Plants

# After the dinosaurs

*Dinosaurs have been extinct for about 65 million years. It is hard after all that time to tell how they lived. But we can compare dinosaurs with some of today's creatures.*

## OUR LANDSCAPE

Humans began to develop two to three million years ago. They never came close to overlapping with the dinosaurs. The Earth we inhabit has less water than in the Mesozoic era. There are fewer horsetails and conifers than before. Grasses now cover large areas of land and there are many more flowering plants. We share our world with numerous different types of creatures including mammals, fishes, reptiles, amphibians and insects. Many have evolved since the age of dinosaurs but there are still some links with that time. Today there are billions of birds, which many scientists think are living relatives of the dinosaurs. And some animals, for example, crocodiles and turtles, have simply stuck around, changing their form only slightly as the millenniums slid by.

## LOOK AGAIN!

Compare this with the Triassic, Jurassic and Cretaceous scenes. What is still alive today?

Bison graze on the grassy plains.

Scientists dig all over the world for the bones of dinosaurs.

45

# Digging for dinosaurs

*Making model dinosaurs from what remains of them is skilful work. Scientists who study fossil evidence are called* **palaeontologists**. *They need help from artists to re-create whole animals.*

**Small bones are wrapped in newspaper and sent back to a laboratory. Larger bones are coated in plaster before the journey.**

## LOOK
### AGAIN!

Look at the *Coelophysis* on pages 10–11. The colours are different. No-one knows the real colours.

**Palaeontologists spend many hours fitting bones together. They often have to model bones to replace ones that are missing.**

**Impressions of skin give some clues about the texture of dinosaurs' bodies. Artists can only guess at their colour and markings from animals alive today.**

· COELOPHYSIS ·

## FOSSIL HUNTING

Finding fossils is hard. First you have to know where to look. Then you must use the right tools to **excavate** the bits and pieces from their surroundings. This is slow, careful work that requires a great deal of patience. Dinosaur digs are often in remote places where camping is uncomfortable. In the early days of digging for dinosaurs, palaeontologists competed with one another to get results. Sometimes mistakes were made, such as the wrong head being put on the wrong body.

**47**

starving
dinosaur

Dating fossilised bones tells us
t many dinosaurs died at
the same time.

udden change in the
mate might have
a drought.

# Why, oh why?

*At the end of the Cretaceous period there was an **extinction** event that wiped out all the dinosaurs and many other animals. Why this happened is still largely unexplained.*

## UNANSWERED QUESTIONS

In the normal course of geological time, species change or die out to allow room for new ones. But every now and then there is a mass extinction event when some of the existing plants and animals disappear more rapidly. After the dinosaurs vanished, mammals were able to develop and diversify into the wide range of types we know today. Many different theories have been suggested for the death of the dinosaurs. Perhaps an absence of natural laxatives clogged their digestive systems? Or something was lacking in their diet to form healthy eggshells? Or all their eggs began hatching into only one sex? Or egg-eating mammals stole too many eggs?

**Some people have even suggested that caterpillars were stripping the vegetation.**

**Some mammals died with the dinosaurs.**

## LOOK AGAIN!

What can you see in the landscape that suggests herbivores were having a hard time?

Meat-eating dinosaurs were probably the last ones to go.

## LOOK AGAIN!

What is happening in this picture that might affect dinosaurs' ability to survive?

Plant seeds can begin to grow again after a very long time.

# So what really happened?

*Nobody knows exactly why the age of dinosaurs ended. A combination of reasons is most likely. They might include extra-terrestrial impact, volcanic activity, spreading diseases and natural extinction.*

### DARK DAYS

One theory for the dinosaur extinction suggests that a giant meteorite collided with the Earth at the end of the Cretaceous period. Spreading red-hot material and the shock waves from the impact would have destroyed animals and vegetation for hundreds of kilometres around. Clouds of steam and choking dust would have blotted out the sun for several years. Without warmth and light, more plants would die. Herbivorous dinosaurs would starve to death. Without prey, meat-eaters were also doomed. **Geologists** know that many volcanoes erupted at the end of the Cretaceous period. They could have produced dust clouds as large and long lasting as a meteorite's impact. During Cretaceous times, sea levels changed and new land bridges formed between continents. Dinosaurs could have mingled and caught each other's diseases. Another view suggests it was just the natural time for dinosaurs to die out.

**Some small mammals survived on limited vegetation or by hibernating.**

# Get the facts on Saurischia

Scientists do not know exactly how many different dinosaurs there were because they are still discovering new types. The Saurischia pictured here represent species in each of the main groups.

Struthiomimus

Saltasaurus

Brachiosaurus

Deinonychus

Ceratosaurus

Coelophysis

Diplodocus

Tyrannosaurus rex

Camarasaurus

Plateosaurus

## SAURISCHIAN PARADE

Saurischia were: theropods (meat-eaters) or sauropods (plant-eaters). They were lizard-hipped. Some moved on two legs; others needed all four to support their weight.

# Get the facts on Ornithischia

*The skeletons of Ornithischia are bird-hipped. Again, some species were bipedal and others were quadrupedal.*

Pachycephalosaurus

Stegosaurus

Euoplocephalus

Hypsilophodon

Hylaeosaurus

Triceratops

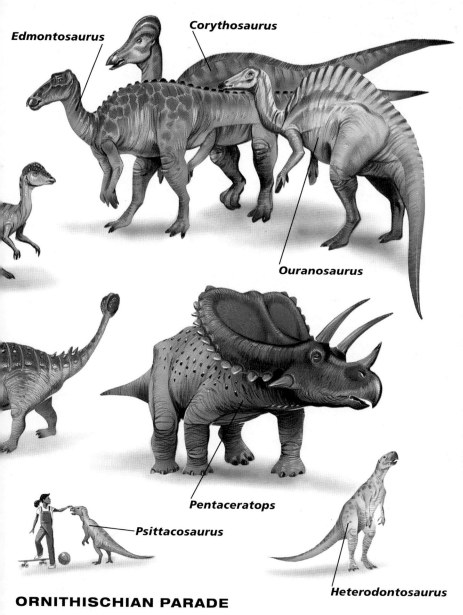

Edmontosaurus

Corythosaurus

Ouranosaurus

Pentaceratops

Psittacosaurus

Heterodontosaurus

## ORNITHISCHIAN PARADE

Ornithischia varied greatly in appearance. Some had clubbed tails and/or armoured skin. Some had horns and/or neck frills. Some had crested or bumpy heads. Some had bony sails or plates along their backs.

# Keeping a pet dino

*The difficulties of keeping a pet dinosaur would be enormous! How would you feed it? Where would it sleep? How would you clean up after it?*

## DINO CARE

At first, hatchlings would be quite small. But remember, dinosaurs grew very fast and doubled in size every two weeks. Your little hatchling would soon outgrow you and would need a huge cage. You would have to bring it big servings of raw meat or plants and buckets full of water. There would be mounds of droppings to clear up—good fertiliser for all the gardens in your neighbourhood. Of course, not all dinosaurs were large. If you chose *Compsognathus* (KOMP-sog-NAT-thus), you would be dealing with a meat-eating animal no larger than a chicken. You might be able to teach a bigger-brained dinosaur some parrot tricks. A talking dinosaur? Now I'd like to see that!

**Even a little meat-eating dinosaur would bite your hand off if you tried to stroke it.**

**Plant-eaters would be less fierce than meat-eaters.**

# Make your own fossil imprint

1. Choose a large shell, leaf or bone.

2. Make up a mixture of plaster of Paris.

3. Smear your object with petroleum jelly to prevent the plaster sticking to it.

4. Place your object in a plastic ice cream tub lined with greaseproof paper.

5. Pour on the plaster and let it set.

6. Remove object from the tray. Turn it over and peel from the plaster. It leaves an impression just as a fossil does.

Do you have space at your place for this dinosaur?

Dinosaur footprints would ruin flowerbeds and lawns.

# GLOSSARY

**bacteria** Tiny organisms.

**bipedal** Standing, walking or running on two legs.

**browse** To eat the leaves of shrubs and trees.

**carnivore** (KAR-niv-or) Eats meat.

**cellulose** The main component of plant cells together with water.

**conifers** Trees or shrubs that bear cones.

**cycads** Low palm-like trees that were widespread in the Mesozoic era and still survive today.

**dicynodont** (die-SIN-oh-dont) Early plant-eating animals.

**embryo** A developing animal yet to be born or hatched.

**evolve** To change through generations. Animals and plants usually evolve to better adapt themselves for the environmental conditions in which they live.

**excavate** To dig out a fossil from a layer of rock.

**extinction** Death of a species of animal or plant.

**extra-terrestrial** Not from the earth; from outer space, for example, meteorites.

**fossil** The remains or imprint of an animal or plant from ancient times that has been preserved in rock.

**frill** The bony shelf that covers the back of the neck of ceratopsids, for example, Triceratops.

**gastroliths** Rounded pebbles found in the stomachs of some animals.

**geologist** A scientist who studies rocks.

**ginkgos** Primitive maidenhair fern trees.

**hatchling** An animal newly hatched from an egg.

**herbivorous** Eats plants.

**horsetails** Primitive plants of the Mesozoic era that look like small bamboo.

**iguana** A tropical lizard with distinctive-shaped teeth.

**incubate** (IN-kew-bate) Keeping an egg at the right temperature for the time between when it is laid and when it hatches (the incubation period).

# GLOSSARY

**mammals** Warm-blooded animals that are usually covered with hair and whose young feed on milk from the mother's teat.

**meteorite** A solid body of rock which crashes into the Earth's surface from space.

**Ornithischia** The group of dinosaurs with bird-like hipbones.

**palaeontologist** (PAY-lee-on-TOL-a-jist) A scientist who studies the evolution of life from fossil evidence.

**predator** An animal that hunts and kills other animals for food.

**prey** An animal that is hunted and killed as food by another animal.

**prosauropod** Ancestor of the sauropods.

**pterosaur** (tair-oh-SORE) Flying reptile of the Mesozoic era.

**quadruped** (KWOD-ra-ped) An animal that stands, walks or runs on four legs.

**reptiles** Animals that do not produce their own body heat, usually lay eggs on land, have scales and have a backbone.

**rhyncosaur** Pig-like reptile with a hooked beak of the late Triassic period.

**Saurischia** The group of dinosaurs with lizard-like hipbones.

**sauropod** Quadrupedal, herbivorous saurischian dinosaur.

**skeleton** The bones of the body that supports the soft tissue.

**species** Kinds of plants and animals.

**thecodonts** The group of reptiles from which the dinosaurs, pterosaurs and crocodiles evolved during the Triassic period.

**theropod** Bipedal, carnivorous saurischian dinosaur.

**trackway** Fossilised footprints.

**vertebra** A spool-shaped bone, many of which join together to form the neck, backbone and tail.

## BOOKS

Baker, Robert, *Dinosaur Heresies,* Longman, Harlow, UK, 1986.

Benton, Michael, *The Best Ever Dinosaur Book,* Kingfisher Books, London, 1998.

Bonnet Wexo, John, *Dinosaurs,* Creative Educaton, Mankato, Minnesota, 1989.

Creagh, Carson, *Dinosaurs,* Discoveries series, Allen & Unwin, Sydney, 1995.

*Dinosaur,* Eyewitness series, Dorling Kindersley, London, 1989.

*Desperate and Deadly Dinosaurs,* Dorling Kindersley, London, 1997.

*Encyclopedia of Dinosaurs,* Beekman House, New York, 1990.

Norman, David, *Dinosaur!,* Boxtree Limited, UK, 1992.

Norman, David, *Illustrated Encyclopedia of Dinosaurs,* Salamander, London, 1985.

Psihoyos, Louis, *Hunting Dinosaurs,* Cassell, London, 1994.

## WEBSITES

DIG Dinosaur Interplanetary Gazette  http:/www.dinosaur.org

Dinosaurs On Line  http://www.dinosauria.com

National Geographic, Dinorama
http://www.nationalgeographic.com/dinorama

The worlds of Mike Keesey, Dinosauricon
http://www.gl.umbc.edu/~tkees1/

## SOCIETIES

The Dinosaur Society
200 Carlton Avenue  East Islip, New York  USA 11730
email: dscociety@aol.com

# INDEX

# INDEX

# INDEX

# FREE

# POSTER!

## Collect all 6 of the gold INVESTIGATE stickers
(you will find one on the stickers' page in each book).

**Send all 6 stickers on a sheet of paper
along with your name and address to:**

Investigate Series Poster
Whitecap Books
351 Lynn Avenue
North Vancouver
British Columbia
V7J 2C4

**and we'll send you your free** INVESTIGATE **series poster.**

Please allow 21 days for delivery.

# COMING SOON

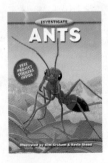
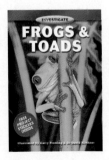